Sally

Lehrwerk für den
Englischunterricht ab Klasse 1

Ausgabe D/E

Pupil's Book 3

Erarbeitet von
Martina Bredenbröcker
Jasmin Brune
Daniela Elsner
Barbara Gleich
Stefanie Gleixner-Weyrauch
Simone Gutwerk
Marion Lugauer
Sabine Schwarz
Anke Spangenberg

Unter Beratung von
Jane Brockmann-Fairchild

Illustriert von
Christine Brand, Wilfried Poll,
Gisela Vogel und Anja Boretzki

Oldenbourg

Inhalt

Special days:

The happy kangaroo song

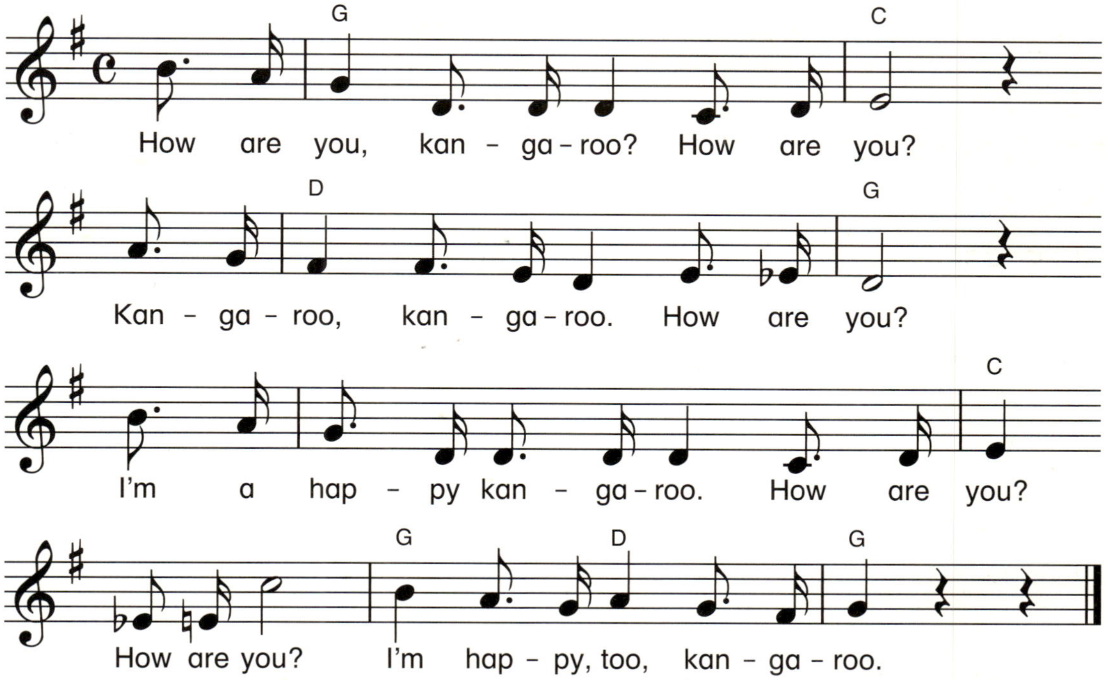

Listen and sing.

English all around

1. Look and speak.

2. There are many English words in the picture.
Make a list.

Mr Blue and Mrs Yellow

1. Listen to the story.
2. What colour is it?

grey
pink
orange
purple
brown
green

Sally's rhyme

One, two, three –
Sally, point to me!

Four, five, six –
Sally, let us mix!

Seven, eight, nine –
now let's stand in line!

Now comes ten,
let's say the rhyme again!

Listen, say the rhyme and do the actions.

In class

1. Listen and point.
2. What school things have you got?
   I've got a …
3. Draw and write. pen

School in England

in class

pupils in school uniform

lunchtime

a lollipop lady

Timetable

	Monday	Tuesday	Wednesday	Thursday	Friday
9.15–9.30	Keep fit	Keep fit	Keep fit	Keep fit	Assembly
9.30–10.30	Maths	Literacy	Maths	Literacy	Drama
10.30–10.45	BREAK	BREAK	BREAK	BREAK	BREAK
10.45–12.15	Literacy	Maths	Literacy	Maths	Music
12.15–1.15	LUNCH	LUNCH	LUNCH	LUNCH	LUNCH
1.15–1.30	Silent reading	Silent reading	Silent reading	Silent reading	Silent reading
1.30–2.45	Art	Science	Project	Science	Rel. education
2.45–3.15	Silent reading	Silent reading	Guitar	Silent reading	Silent reading
3.15–3.30	HOME	HOME	HOME	HOME	HOME

Look at the photos.

Snakes and ladders

Roll the dice. Do the actions.

Correct action: Go up the ladder.

Wrong action: Go down the snake.

Sally's hotspot:

Correct action: Roll the dice again.

Wrong action: Go back to the start.

3 Touch your head.

8 Bend your knees.

16 Sing: Head and shoulders …

19 Wash your hands.

24 Count your fingers.

27 Shake your feet.

29 Stretch your arms.

33 Point to your eyes.

43 Touch your ears.

48 Stretch your legs.

52 Brush your hair.

58 Open your mouth and say: Good morning!

59 Point to your nose.

62 Shake your body.

Glad monster, sad monster

1. Listen, point and speak. The yellow monster is …
2. Draw your own monster and write. My monster is …

At the bazaar

1. Listen and ask your partner. How much is the …?

2. You have got £3. What can you buy? Make a list.

Sally in the snow

Look and speak. Sally puts on her …
Sally takes off her …

Sally go round the sun

Monday Tuesday Wednesday Thursday

Friday Saturday Sunday

1. Listen and sing.
2. What day is it today? Today is …
3. Write down the days of the week.

The weather forecast

1. Listen and point.
2. What's the weather like today?
3. Make a weather chart for one week.
   On Monday it's ...

The more we get together

The more we get together, together, together, the more we get together, the happier we are. I'm your friend. You're my friend. I'm your friend. You're my friend. The more we get together, the happier we are.

Listen, sing and dance.

My family

my mum and dad

my brother Tim

my grandma and grandpa

Can you find my dad?

aunt Helen

Can you find my mum and Tim?

Can you find my grandma and grandpa?

Can you find aunt Helen?

Look and point.

Sally's birthday cake

Sally is having a birthday party. She gets a birthday cake.

Sally is very happy. She jumps up high.

Oh dear! The cake is on the floor.

Sally slips. She falls on her cake. What a mess!

But look, what's that? There is a penny in the cake.

1. Look and read.
2. Write a birthday card to Sally.

Drinks

What is it? tea, coke, orange juice, coffee, hot chocolate, milk

1. Look and guess.

What drinks do you like?

Emily likes orange juice.
She doesn't like coffee.
Phil likes tea.
He doesn't like milk.

2. Read and speak.

The magic trick

Do the trick.

My favourite breakfast

breakfast on a school day

breakfast on Sunday

1. Look and speak.

Do you like  on your / in your 

?

2. Ask your partner.

3. What do you have for breakfast?
For breakfast I have ...

The lemon tree

2. Here we go round the cherry tree …
3. Here we go round the apple tree …
4. Here we go round the orange tree …

Listen, sing and dance.

Let's make some lemonade!

At the market

1. Listen and speak.
2. Make a shopping list for your fruit salad.
3. Tell your partner. I'd like …

Little dog lost

Listen. Where is Bobby?

These pets have new homes

Jack and Mr Tailor

Tippy and Mrs Davis

Rocky and Sammy Baker

Hopsy and Sophie Miller

Molly and Kevin Fisher

Fred and Alice Smith

Charlie and Mrs Cooper

1. Listen, look and speak.
2. Do a class survey.

Speedy

From tadpole to frog

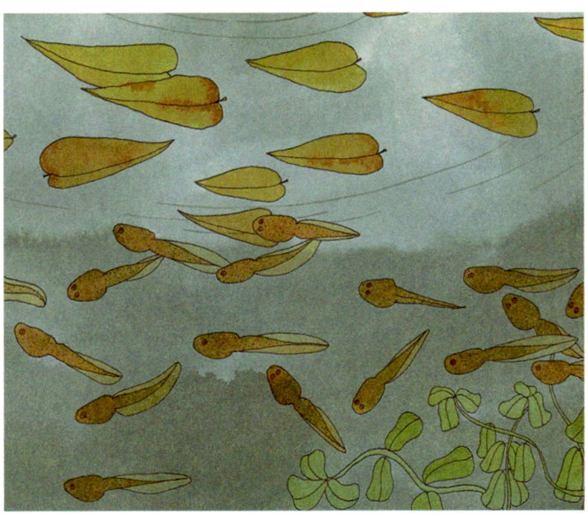

Listen and look.

Froggy comic

Let's go to London!

the Royal Family

guards

Buckingham Palace

a double-decker bus

the London Eye

Madame Tussaud's

Look at the photos.

On the farm

1. Look and name the farm animals. Count them.

2. Where are the animals?

Alphabet rhyme

A B C D E F G,
on the farm there is a bee.

H I J K L M N,
it lands directly on a hen.

O P Q R S T U,
and asks her friendly: “How are you?”

V W X Y Z,
“I'm fine, but please, get off my head.”

1. Listen and point.
2. Read the rhyme.

On the beach

1. Look and speak. How many seashells can you find?
2. Draw your own summer picture and write words on it.
   sun, beach, sea, beach ball, ice cream ...

Robin Hood's game

Robin Hood
Look!
The sheriff is coming.
Go to 16.
16
17
18
19
20
21
22
23
ook at
e castle.
oll the dice again.
Hide behind
the tree.
Go to 19.
Have breakfast
on the farm.
Miss a turn.
Wave to the farmer.
Go to 37.
33
34
35
36
37
Drink some milk.
Go to 34.
38
32
31
30
29
28
27
Give money to the poor.
Go to 31.
39
40
41
42
FINISH

It's Halloween

1. Listen to the song.
2. Listen to the story.

Rush hour

The ghost

I saw a ghost.
He saw me, too.
I waved at him.
But he said "Boo!".

Tongue twister

Two witches are watching two watches.
Which witch is watching which watch?

Look and read.
Can you say the tongue twister?

Christmas Eve

I hear them

1. What day is it?
   What are Tim and Susan waiting for?
2. Sing the song.
3. Make a Christmas card.

Make your own Christmas stocking!

You need:
thick brown paper,
a pencil,
scissors,
glue,
a hole punch,
wool,
felt tips or wax crayons

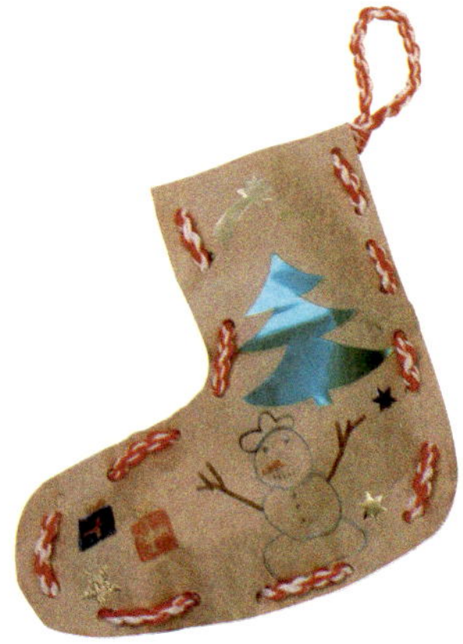

1
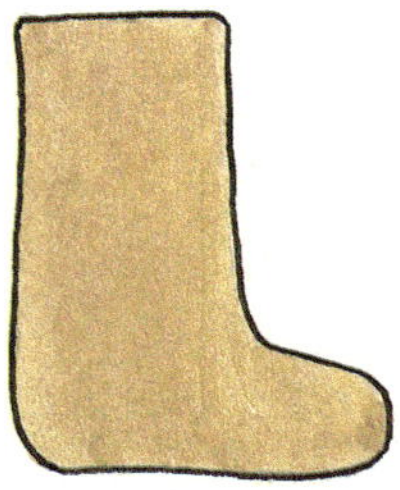

2
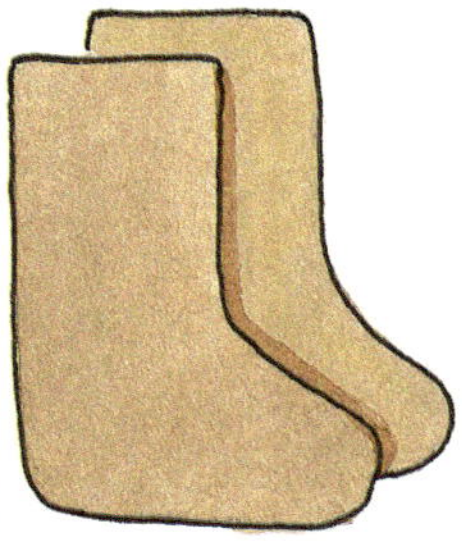

Draw a large stocking on the thick brown paper.
Cut out two copies of the stocking.

3

Glue the two stockings together around the edges.
Leave the top open.

4

5

Punch holes around the edges of the stocking.
Weave wool in and out of the holes.
Leave a loop of wool at one end and tie it into a knot.

6

Decorate your stocking.

Valentine's cards

Candy is sweet,
this is true,
but for my Valentine
I'll choose you.

Jingle, jangle,
silver bangle,
you look fit
from every angle.

I like you!

Roses are red,
violets are blue,
sugar is sweet
and so are you!

Look and read.
What's your favourite rhyme?

Let's make an Easter-egg cup!

You need:
a toilet roll,
white paper,
pink paper,
glue,
scissors,
felt tips or coloured pencils,
pipe cleaners

Cover the toilet roll with white paper.

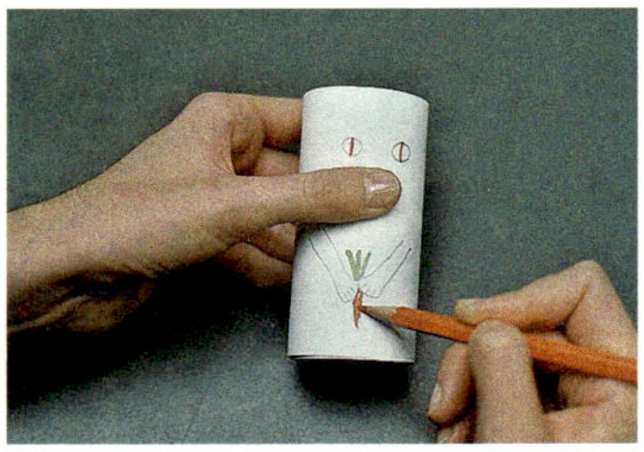

Draw a bunny face on it.

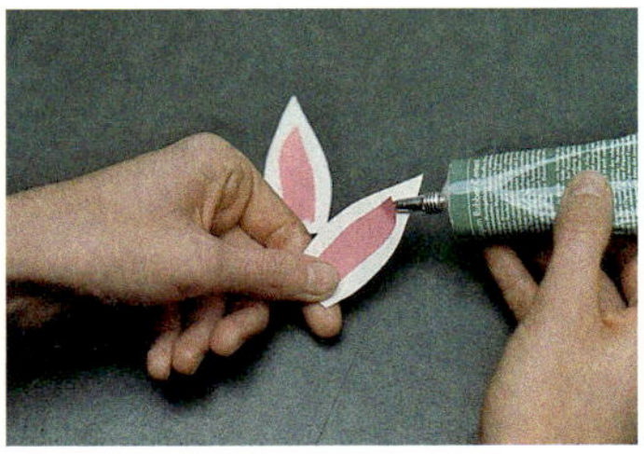

Cut out two ears from the white paper and the centres from the pink paper.

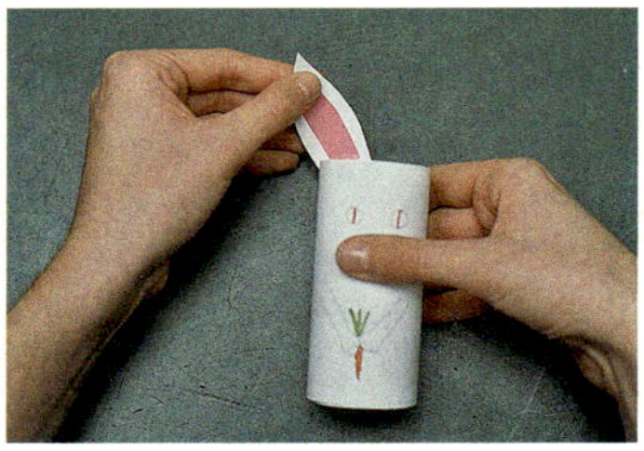

Glue on the ears.

Glue on the pipe cleaners.

Words

Africa Afrika
America Amerika
angry wütend
animal das Tier
animal centre das Tierheim
apple der Apfel
April der April
arm der Arm
arrow der Pfeil
Asia Asien
August der August
aunt die Tante
Australia Australien
autumn der Herbst
away weg

bacon der Speck
ball der Ball
banana die Banane
basket der Korb
bat die Fledermaus
beach der Strand
beach ball der Wasserball
behind hinter
to bend beugen
big groß
bird der Vogel
birthday der Geburtstag
black schwarz
blue blau
board die Tafel
body der Körper
book das Buch
boot der Stiefel
bow der Bogen
box die Schachtel
boy der Junge, der Bub
bread das Brot
breakfast das Frühstück
brother der Bruder
brown braun
to brush bürsten
budgie der Wellensittich
bus der Bus
butter die Butter
to buy kaufen

cake der Kuchen
Canada Kanada
candle die Kerze
cap die Kappe
car das Auto
card die Karte
carrot die Karotte, die Möhre
castle die Burg
cat die Katze
to catch fangen
chalk die Kreide
cheap billig
cherry die Kirsche
child das Kind
children die Kinder
chimney der Schornstein
Christmas Weihnachten
Christmas tree
der Weihnachtsbaum, der Christbaum
to clap klatschen
to clean putzen
clothes die Kleidung

cloud die Wolke
cloudy bewölkt
coat der Mantel
coffee der Kaffee
coke die Cola
cold kalt
colour die Farbe
to colour anmalen
computer der Computer
computer game das Computerspiel
cookie der Keks
cornflakes die Cornflakes
costume die Verkleidung
to count zählen
cousin der Cousin, die Cousine
cow die Kuh
cup die Tasse
to cut schneiden

to dance tanzen
dark dunkel
day der Tag
December der Dezember
desk der Schreibtisch
dice der Würfel
dirty schmutzig
to do magic zaubern
dog der Hund
doll die Puppe
door die Tür
down hinunter
to draw zeichnen
dress das Kleid
drink das Getränk
duck die Ente

ear das Ohr
Easter Ostern
Easter bunny der Osterhase
Easter egg das Osterei
egg das Ei
England England
Europe Europa
exercise die Übung
expensive teuer
eye das Auge

fairy die Fee
family die Familie
farm animal das Bauernhoftier
father der Vater
Father Christmas
der Weihnachtsmann
favourite (pet) Lieblings(tier)
February der Februar
feet die Füße
to fill füllen
fine gut, schön
finger der Finger
fish der Fisch, die Fische
flower die Blume
fly die Fliege
to fly fliegen
fog der Nebel
foggy nebelig
folder der Schnellhefter
food das Essen
foot der Fuß
forest der Wald
Friday der Freitag

friend der Freund, die Freundin
friendly freundlich
frog der Frosch
fruit die Frucht, das Obst
fruit salad der Obstsalat

game das Spiel
to get up aufstehen
ghost der Geist
girl das Mädchen
glue der Kleber
to go gehen, fahren
good gut
goose die Gans
grandfather der Großvater
grandmother die Großmutter
grass das Gras
Great Britain Großbritannien
green grün
grey grau
guard die Wache
guinea pig das Meerschweinchen

hair das Haar
Halloween Halloween
ham der Schinken
hamster der Hamster
hand die Hand
happy glücklich
hat der Hut
head der Kopf
hen die Henne
holidays die Ferien
honey der Honig
horse das Pferd
hot chocolate der Kakao
hot heiß
hungry hungrig

ice cream das Eis
in front of vor
in in
inline skates die Inlineskates
insect das Insekt

jacket die Jacke
jam die Marmelade
January der Januar
jeans die Jeans
July der Juli
to jump springen
June der Juni

kangaroo das Känguru
king der König
knee das Knie
to knock klopfen
to know wissen, kennen

ladder die Leiter
leaf (leaves) das Blatt (die Blätter)
leg das Bein

lemon die Zitrone
to like mögen
to listen (to) zuhören
little klein
to live leben

March der März
market der Markt
May der Mai
meadow die Wiese
melon die Melone
mice die Mäuse
milk die Milch
mitten der Fäustling
Monday der Montag
money das Geld
month der Monat
monster das Ungeheuer
moon der Mond
morning der Morgen
mother die Mutter
mouse die Maus
mouth der Mund
to move (sich) bewegen

name der Name
New Zealand Neuseeland
next to neben
night die Nacht
nose die Nase
November der November
number die Zahl

October der Oktober
old alt
on auf
orange die Orange; orange
orange juice der Orangensaft

to paint malen
palace der Palast
parents die Eltern
to pay bezahlen
pear die Birne
pen der Füller
pencil der Bleistift
pencil case das Mäppchen
people die Leute
pepper der Pfeffer
pet das Haustier
picture das Bild
pig das Schwein
pineapple die Ananas
pink rosa
to play spielen
please bitte
plum die Pflaume
pond der Teich
poor arm
present das Geschenk
prince der Prinz
princess die Prinzessin
pullover der Pullover
pumpkin der Kürbis
purple lila
to put setzen, stellen, legen
to put on anziehen

queen die Königin

rabbit das Kaninchen
rain der Regen
rainy regnerisch
to read lesen
red rot
reindeer das Rentier, die Rentiere
rich reich
roll das Brötchen, die Semmel
rubber der Radiergummi
ruler das Lineal

sad traurig
salt das Salz
sand der Sand
Saturday der Samstag
scared erschrocken, ängstlich
scarf der Schal
school die Schule
schoolbag die Schultasche
scissors die Schere
sea das Meer
seashell die Muschel
season die Jahreszeit
to see sehen
to sell verkaufen
September der September
to shake schütteln
sheep das Schaf
sheriff der Sheriff
to shine scheinen
shoe der Schuh
short kurz
shorts die kurze Hose
shoulder die Schulter
to show zeigen
to sing singen
sister die Schwester
skirt der Rock
sleigh der (Pferde-)Schlitten
slow langsam
small klein
snake die Schlange
to snorkel schnorcheln, tauchen
snow der Schnee
snowman der Schneemann
snowy verschneit
sock die Socke
song das Lied
spaceship das Raumschiff
to speak sprechen
spider die Spinne
spoon der Löffel
spring der Frühling
to stamp stampfen
star der Stern
stocking der Strumpf
strong stark
sugar der Zucker
summer der Sommer
sun die Sonne
Sunday der Sonntag
sunglasses die Sonnenbrille
sunny sonnig
sweatshirt das Sweatshirt
sweet süß
sweets die Süßigkeiten
to swim schwimmen

tadpole die Kaulquappe
to take nehmen
to take off ausziehen
tall groß
tea der Tee
teddy bear der Teddybär
teeth die Zähne
thirsty durstig
Thursday der Donnerstag
tired müde
toast der Toast
toe der Zeh
tooth der Zahn
tortoise die Schildkröte
to touch anfassen
towel das Handtuch
toy das Spielzeug
tree der Baum
trousers die Hose
T-shirt das T-Shirt
Tuesday der Dienstag

uncle der Onkel
under unter
Union Jack britische Fahne
United States of America die Vereinigten Staaten von Amerika, die USA
up hinauf

Valentine's Day der Valentinstag

to write schreiben
warm warm
water das Wasser
to wash waschen
wax figure die Wachsfigur
to wear tragen
weather das Wetter
weather forecast die Wettervorhersage
Wednesday der Mittwoch
white weiß
wind der Wind
windy windig
winter der Winter
witch die Hexe
woolly hat die Mütze
workbook das Arbeitsheft

yellow gelb

Quellenverzeichnis

3 The happy kangaroo song, reproduced by permission of Oxford University Press, from: Children's Jazz Chants Old & New Student's Book by Carolyn Graham, © Oxford University Press, 2004
9 Fotos: (1) Adam Butler/dpa-Bildarchiv; (2) Niki Mareschal/gettyimages; (3) Jenny Woodcock, Reflections Photolibrary/Corbis; (4) MetroFrosh
12 Glad monster, sad monster by Anne Miranda and Ed Emberley (Ill.), © 1997 Boston Little, Brown and Company
21 Fotos: André Roth/picbyte
23 Fotos: Johann Jilka,
24 Fotos: Heiko Jegodtka, München
28 From tadpole to frog by Wendy Pfeffer and Holly Keller, illustrations copyright © 1994 by Holly Keller, used by permission of HarperCollins Publishers, New York
30 Fotos: (1) Ullsteinbild-AP/Pool; (2) ASK/Visum; (3) Alamy Images; (4) Jan Butchofsky-Houser/ Corbis; (5) Ask/Visum; (6) Jahreszeiten Verlag (Jan Brettschneider)
37 Rush hour, nach: Schul-Jugendzeitschrift O!kay!, Ausgabe November 1998, Domino Verlag, München
42 Fotos: Heiko Jegodtka, München

Trotz entsprechender Bemühungen ist es nicht in allen Fällen gelungen, den Copyrightinhaber ausfindig zu machen. Gegen Nachweis der Rechte zahlt der Verlag für die Abdruckerlaubnis die gesetzlich geschuldete Vergütung.

www.oldenbourg-bsv.de

Das Papier ist aus chlorfrei gebleichtem Zellstoff hergestellt, ist säurefrei und recyclingfähig.

1. Auflage 2009

Druck 13 12 11 10 09
Die letzte Zahl bezeichnet das Jahr des Drucks.
Alle Drucke dieser Auflage sind untereinander unverändert und im Unterricht nebeneinander verwendbar.

Umschlagkonzept: Mendell & Oberer, München
Umschlag: Dietmar Schell, unter Verwendung einer Illustration von Wilfried Poll
Lektorat: Salomé Dick, Berlin; Ursula Händl-Sagawe
Herstellung: Jutta Creutzburg
Layout und Satz: artesmedia GmbH, Grasbrunn
Illustrationen: Christine Brand, Wilfried Poll, Gisela Vogel, Anja Boretzki
Reproduktion: Repro Ludwig GmbH, Zell am See
Druck: Himmer AG, Augsburg

ISBN 978-3-637-00439-9

ISBN 978-3-637-00439-9

Oldenbourg